1

Games

How to play more than 60 of the world's greatest travel games for two or more players

JOE GANNON

Mud Puddle inc.
NEW YORK

Travel Games:
How to play more than 60 of the world's greatest
travel games for two or more players
by Joe Gannon

Mud Puddle Books, Inc.
36 W. 25th St.
New York, NY 10010
info@mudpuddleinc.com

ISBN: 978-1-60311-221-5

Book design by Mulberry Tree Press, Inc.

Printed and bound in China

Contents

Introduction

You're headed off on that long drive to Florida, or flight to the islands. Everyone is looking forward to the excitement and adventure of getting away. Well, there's no reason to wait for arrival at your destination to start the fun. With all the wonderful entertaining travel games that have been invented over the years, you can fill the hours in transit with playful diversion—and you'll never have to hear that common refrain, "Mommy, are we there yet?"

Guessing Games

Guessing games are among the oldest and most loved of all travel games. They require no equipment except your wits and logic, and can wisk you away for countless hours of entertainment.

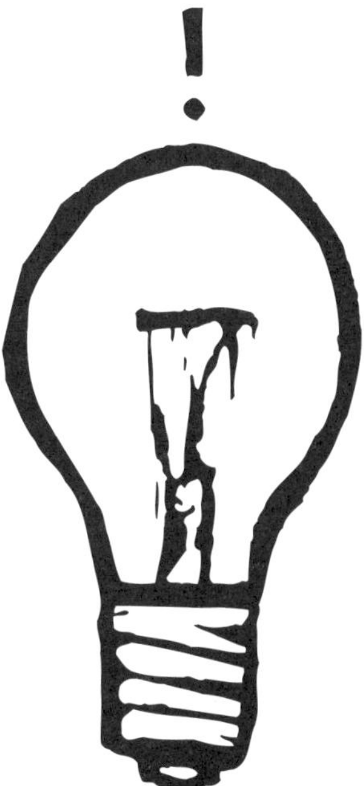

Twenty Questions

1. One player thinks of a person, place or thing and tells the others whether it is animal, vegetable or mineral.

   Animal includes people or animals—living or dead, real or fictional—as well as anything made from an animal—such as a leather jacket, or a part of an animal—like a moose's antlers. It could also be a group of people or animals—like a herd of sheep, or the cast of a movie.

   Vegetable includes any plant—like a carrot or a tree, as well anything made from a plant—like a cotton tablecloth or a loaf of bread.

   Mineral pretty much covers everything else—rocks, minerals, metals, plastics, water, oil, etc., and things made of such materials—like the Rocky Mountains, Lake Erie, a pair of dice, or a cruise ship.

   Try to pick something that fits completely into one of the categories. Mostly, that will mean avoiding things that combine vegetable and mineral—like most houses, which will be made from wood (vegetable) on a concrete (mineral) foundation. But it's OK to use things that fit primarily into one of the categories—like the leather jacket, even though it probably has metal snaps or zippers, or plastic buttons.

2. The other players are allowed twenty yes-or-no questions to figure out what the answer is. The questions may be answered "yes," "no," "sometimes," or "partially."

3. If the answer is "no," play moves to the next player in turn. With any other answer the player may continue.

4. In variations on the game, the players may be eliminated if they guess wrong, or they may be allowed to guess once on each turn for which their question was answered "yes," and then continue without penalty, even if their guess is wrong. This needs to be established before the game begins.

5. The first player to correctly guess the person, place or thing is the winner.

Strategy tip: Try to start with broad questions—the best question will eliminate half of the remaining possibilities. As you narrow the field of choices, you then ask more and more specific questions, each time trying to reduce the possibilities by about half. This strategy will allow you to determine the answer as quickly as possible. It can also be useful to remember the tendencies of the player making the selection. For instance, you may notice that they often select specific movie stars when the category is animal, or sports equipment when the category is mineral. If you notice such a tendency you can adjust your questions accordingly, and possibly find a shortcut to the answer.

Other guessing games similar to Twenty Questions:

Who Am I?

1. The chooser pretends to be a famous person that all of the players should be familiar with.
2. The players, each in turn, ask yes-or-no questions.

   For example:

   "Are you in the performing arts?"
   "Are you in politics?"
   "Are you in sports?"
   "Are you in the media?"
   And so on . . .
3. If the answer is yes, the player may ask another question. If he thinks he knows the answer, his question may be a guess at who the person is.
4. If the answer is no, play moves to the next player in turn.
5. The first player to correctly identify the chosen person is the winner.
6. You may set a limit on the number of rounds of questions, or you may choose to continue the game until the correct answer has been found.

Variation: You may decide to allow the chooser to select any person that all of the players will know. Family and friends would then be added to the pool of possible answers.

Other guessing games similar to Twenty Questions:

What's My Line?

1. The chooser pretends to be in a chosen line of work or profession that all of the players should be familiar with.
2. The players, each in turn, ask yes-or-no questions.

   For example:

   "Do you supply a product or a service?"
   "Is your enterprise profit-making or non-profit?"
   "Do you wear a uniform in your profession?"
   And so on . . .
3. If the answer is yes, the player may ask another question. If she thinks she knows the answer, her question may be a guess at what the line of work is.
4. If the answer is no, play moves to the next player in turn.
5. The first player to correctly identify the chosen profession is the winner.
6. You may set a limit on the number of rounds of questions, or you may choose to continue the game until the correct answer has been found.

Other guessing games similar to Twenty Questions:

What Animal Am I?

1. The chooser pretends to be an animal with characteristics the players should be familiar with.
2. The players, each in turn, ask yes-or-no questions.

   For example:
   "Do you have fur?"
   "Do you have feathers?"
   "Do you walk on four legs?"
   "Do you live in the forest?"
   And so on . . .

3. If the answer is yes, the player may make ask another question. If he thinks he knows the answer, his question may be a guess at what the animal is.
4. If the answer is no, play moves to the next player in turn.
5. The first player to guess the chosen animal is the winner.
6. You may set a limit on the number of rounds of questions, or you may choose to continue the game until the correct answer has been found.

Other guessing games similar to Twenty Questions:

What Am I Eating?

1. The chooser selects a food that all of the players should be familiar with.
2. The players, each in turn, ask yes-or-no questions.

   For example:
   "Is what you are eating an animal product or a plant product?"
   "Is what you are eating sweet?"
   "Is it chewy?"
   And so on . . .

3. If the answer is yes, the player may make ask another question. If she thinks she knows the answer, her question may be a guess at what the food is.
4. If the answer is no, play moves to the next player in turn.
5. The first player to guess the chosen food is the winner.
6. You may set a limit on the number of rounds of questions, or you may choose to continue the game until the correct answer has been found.

Botticelli

Botticelli is one of the most complex guessing games and may prove frustrating to younger players.

1. One player, or team, starts the game as the chooser and thinks of the name of a famous person—real or fictional, living or dead.
2. The chooser states the first letter of the famous person's last name to the other players.
3. In turn, the other players, or team, must try to determine the identity of the famous person by first making a guess as to who the subject might be, and then asking a question to try and confirm their guess.
4. The chooser must answer yes or no, and make reference to some famous person who meets the criteria being asked about. That is, the answer need not refer to the hidden identity that the players are trying to guess if there is another famous person that meets the criteria. See examples for clarification.

5. A question may only be asked once, so any future question about the same trait or characteristic must include some other trait as well. If the same question is asked again, it is disqualified and play moves to the next guesser.

The following examples are best used to explain this somewhat complex process:

The chosen famous identity might be Johann Sebastian Bach. The letter "B" would be announced.

Based on "B." the questioner might guess that the chosen identity could well be the very obvious "Botticelli."

If so, she might ask, "Are you a famous artist?"

The chooser could then answer, "No, I am not Sandro Boticelli," or just as easily, "No, I am not William Blake." These answers are true, and reference a famous person who meets the criteria, in this case, a famous artist whose name begins with "B." Play would then move to the next guesser.

If the chooser cannot think of someone famous who meets the criteria, he would answer, "No, and I don't know who you are referring to." The guesser would then ask directly about their guessed identity, "Are you Sandro Boticelli?" If she has guessed correctly she wins the game. If not, she may then ask a simple yes-or-no question to further narrow the choices–for example, "Are you real or fictional?" There are many other good general yes-or-no questions that can narrow the field of possible choices: "Are you male or female?" or, "Are you dead or alive?" (A fictional character is deemed to be dead if they have died in the fictional work. If they are still alive at the end of the work they are deemed to be alive for the purpose of this question.)

If the answer is yes, she may think of another identity and ask about another descriptive characteristic; for instance, thinking of Yogi Berra, "Are you a famous baseball catcher?" and so on, until she receives a "no" answer and the turn passes.

Or, based on "B," the questioner might guess that the chosen identity could be the famous composer Ludwig von Beethoven.

If so, she might ask, "Are you a famous composer?"

The guesser has correctly guessed a trait of the chosen identity, but the chooser need not confirm that fact as long as he can think of another famous person who fits the criteria asked about. In this case, the chooser could answer, "No, I am not Ludwig von Beethoven," or just as easily, "No, I am not Johannes Brahms." Note that composers have not been ruled out, but the simple question "Are you a famous composer?" cannot be asked again. The next time the guesser might ask

"Are you a famous composer who is deaf?" By adding a trait to the question, it becomes permissible.

If, however, the chooser had not been able to think of another famous composer's name starting with "B," he would have to answer "Yes, but I am not sure who you are referring to." The guesser would then ask directly, "Are you Ludwig von Beethoven?" While the answer will be "No, I am not Ludwig von Beethoven," the guessers will now have confirmed the crucial information that the identity is definitely that of a famous composer whose name begins with "B."

That would likely lead the next guesser to ask the previously suggested and more restrictive question, "Are you a famous composer who is deaf?" With that, the round would be completed in very short order.

6. The guesser who forces the chooser to reveal the hidden identity is the winner of the round and becomes the next chooser.

In team play:

1. Teams alternate the roles of chooser and guesser in each round.
2. A point is awarded to the guessing team each time the questioning passes to another player on the team.
3. Players within a team are allowed to consult with each other before guessing or answering.
4. A game should include an equal number of rounds as chooser and guesser for each of the teams.
5. The team with the lowest score at the end of play is the winner.

Variations:

Bratislava • same rules but with places instead of people.
Vermicelli • same rules but with types of food instead of people.
Protozoa • same rules but with types of living things instead of people.

Coffee Pot

1. The chooser picks a verb.
2. Players ask yes-or-no questions but substitute the words "coffee pot" in place of the secret verb in their questions.

   For example:
   "Would I be allowed to coffee pot at school?"
   "If I were coffee potting with my friends would they think I was strange?"
   "Did you coffee pot today?"
   And so on . . .

3. If the answer is yes, the player may ask another question. If he thinks he knows the answer his question may be a guess at what the verb is.
4. If the answer is no, play moves to the next player in turn.
5. The first player to correctly guess the verb is the winner.

Grandma Is Strange

1. The chooser selects some criterion by which "Grandma" will decide if she likes something or not.

2. The chooser makes a pair of statements describing things that "Grandma" likes or dislikes based on that criterion.

   For example, "My Grandma likes cherries but she doesn't like bananas."

3. Each in turn, the other players ask about what Grandma might like.

4. The first player might ask, "Does she like blueberries?"

   If the chooser has selected "things that are red" as the criteria, she might respond, "No, she doesn't like blueberries, but she does like raspberries." Thus, whenever answering no, the chooser must always add something that fits the criteria as a further example. Since the answer was no, play moves to the next guesser.

   If the chooser had selected "words with a double-r" as the criteria, she might respond, "Yes, she likes blueberries." The questioning player could then take one guess at what the criteria might be, because players are allowed one guess at the criteria after each "yes" answer that they receive. If he guesses the right criteria he wins, and the round is over. If he guess wrong he may then ask another question to try to determine what similarity between cherries and blueberries forms the hidden criteria.

5. The first player to correctly ascertain the criteria for what "grandma" likes is the winner.

Name That Tune

❶ The chooser selects a song that all of the players should be familiar with.

❷ The chooser hums the tune loud enough for all of the players to hear.

If you want to make the game a little easier, the chooser will announce the musical genre of the selected song–for, example: rock, pop, blues, classical, and so on . . .

❸ The first player to recognize the song and name it is the winner.

You may also decide to allow identification by first line, etc. to make it easier for players who may not know the actual title of the song.

Variation: In an alternative for non-hummers, the chooser taps out the tune of the song until someone recognizes and names it. This variation works surprisingly well. If you play this variation all of the choosers should tap out the tune to keep the game fair.

I See Something

1. Pick out an object in plain sight of all of the players with some namable characteristic.
2. Start the game by saying "I see something (name the characteristic)"—for instance, "I see something blue," or, "I see something wooden."
3. In turn, the other players try to guess the object by naming something that fits the descriptive characteristic.
4. You then reply yes or no. If the answer is no you also describe how close the guesser's object is to the target object by telling the guesser if they are warm or cold, or getting hotter/getting colder.

   For instance, if the object he guesses is across the room from the target object you would say, "No, you're very cold." If the next player guesses and the object they select is closer to the target object, you would say, "No, but you're getting warmer." If he selects an object right next to the target object, you would say, "No, but you're very hot."
5. The first player to correctly identify the selected object is the winner.

Search Games

Search games bring in the scenery and involve the players in their surroundings. They are also some of the simpler games and so are suitable for young children as well.

License Plate Bingo

1. Make up bingo cards like these with pencil and paper.
2. Randomly insert two-digit number combinations in each of the squares on each card. (diagrams)
3. When you see a number combination on a passing license plate that matches one on your card. Call it out, and circle it on your card.
4. Anyone else who has it may circle it as well.
5. The first one circle all the combinations in a complete row—up/down, across, or diagonally—is the winner.

25	17	64	98
37	24	58	22
62	97	61	91
47	33	39	87

25	17	64	98
37	24	58	22
62	97	61	91
47	33	39	87

25	17	64	98
37	24	58	22
62	97	61	91
47	33	39	87

25	17	64	98
37	24	58	22
62	97	61	91
47	33	39	87

Alphabet Derby

❶ Race to see who can find all the letters in the alphabet in sequence in license plates, traffic signs and other roadside signs, billboards, etc.

❷ ***There are several constraints that can be added to make the race last:***

You may limit the types of signs or other objects on which to look for the letters. For instance, you may choose to use only traffic signs and not commercial signs. Or, you may choose to use only the lettering on trucks. Or, you may choose to use only the letters on license plates.

You may choose to allow only "first letters." So a letter must be the first letter on the license plate, or the first letter in a word on a sign, etc. in order to be used.

You may decide to play silently allowing all players who see an instance of a letter to use it. Or you may choose to play with letter claiming, where the first player to call out a letter and its location "owns" it and the other players must find their own.

❸ The first player to complete the full alphabet is the winner.

Car Collector

1. See who can collect the most different car makes.
2. The first one to spot and recognize a particular vehicle calls out the make, claims it and is awarded the points.
3. If you'd like, you can make the game more difficult by requiring players to correctly name the make and model in order to be awarded the points–for example, Ford Taurus, or Honda Civic.
4. In heavy traffic it may be best to eliminate the entire 1-point section of makes and only search for the higher value ones.
5. The player with the most points at the end of play is the winner.

Here is a fairly complete list of car makes from manufacturers around the world with a point system for keeping score.

1 POINT EACH
Buick
Cadillac
Chevrolet
Chrysler
Dodge
Ford
GMC
Honda
Hyundai
Isuzu
Jeep
Kia
Lincoln
Mazda
Mercury
Mitsubishi
Nissan
Pontiac
Saturn
Scion
Subaru
Suzuki
Toyota
Volkswagen

2 POINTS EACH
Acura
Audi
BMW
Daewoo
Fuji
HUMMER
Infiniti
Jaguar
Land Rover
Lexus
Mercedes Benz
MINI
Porsche
Saab
Volvo

5 POINTS EACH
Aston Martin
Bentley
Bugatti
Ferrari
Lamborghini
Lotus
Maserati
Rolls-Royce

10 POINTS EACH
custom cars and antiques of any make

Variation: Motorcycle Collector–play the same but with makes and models of motorcycles.

License Plate Numbers

1. Play begins with ready-set-GO
2. The players must find the numbers 1 through 25 on the license plates of passing cars
3. The numbers must be found in sequence
4. Only one number may be counted from a single license plate

Finding 1 through 9 is pretty easy compared to finding 10 through 25, for which the two digits must be found in sequence on the same plate.

5. You may decide to play silently allowing all players who see an instance of a number to use it. Or you may choose to play with number claiming, where the first player to call out a number and its location "owns" it and the other players must find their own.
6. The first player to find all twenty-five numbers in sequence is the winner.

License Plate Poker

1. To deal a hand each player randomly picks a license plate from a passing car. Optionally, pick two plates per player to make better opening poker hands.
2. The cars should be selected while they are passing, before the plates can be read.
3. Players write down their hands, the numbers and letters on the plates, and then create the best 5-card poker hand they can using the following card values:

   numbers 1-9 count as themselves
   a zero counts as a 10,
   and the letters J, Q, K, & A are Jack, Queen, King, and Ace
   other letters don't count for anything unless you want to designate one of them as a wild card
4. There are no suits in License Plate Poker so you can't draw a flush. However, this variety does allow for the unlikely but possible five-of-a-kind.

The value ranking of possible hands is as follows:

five-of-a-kind

four-of-a-kind

full house

straight

three-of-a-kind

two pairs

one pair

high card

Variation: You may include an option to draw additional cards by selecting another plate at random. With the draw option a player must cross out the numbers and letters that she wants to discard from the first plate. She must be left with no more than 4 numbers/letters that she is still to use. In making her hand, she MUST use those numbers from the first plate that are not crossed out. Numbers and letters from the second plate can only be used to fill out the hand. For example, if a player keeps a 2-3-4-5 hand and crosses out the rest of the numbers and letters (looking for a straight), she is only allowed to use one of the numbers from the second plate in making her hand. If on the other hand she had chosen to keep a 4-4 hand and cross out all of the other characters (looking to add to a pair), she would be allowed to use any three characters from the new plate.

License Plate Word Search

1. Decide on a target word, a fairly long one is best.
2. Players must look for the letters of the word in the license plates of passing cars.
3. The first one to see a letter may call it out and claim it for their use.
4. The other players may not use it, they must find their own.
5. The first player to find all of the letters in the word is the winner.

Variation: Normally the letters need not be found in sequence, but if you want to make the game last longer you can add that requirement.

Sight Seeing

1. Pick something that you are liable to see along the way.
2. For instance, you might pick cows if you're in the country or fire hydrants if you're in the city.
3. When a player spots one he or she calls out and claims it for their score.
4. Keep track of how many each player spots first.
5. The one with the most at the end of the game is the winner.
6. You can set a time limit, or just make the game last for the time between rest stops.

Common items that can be the object of your search:

cows

horses

dogs

cats

fire hydrants

billboards

gas stations

bicyclists

joggers

fast-food restaurants

Road Sign Search

1. Players search for particular types of traffic signs.
2. First you make a search list that is supplied to all of the players.
3. Players search for a particular sequence of traffic signs, having to find, claim, and cross each off the list in sequence.
4. You can adapt the list to suit the varieties of signs that you are likely to encounter along the trip you are taking.
5. The first player to spot a particular sign from the list calls it out and claims it as his own. The other players must then find their own instances of the sign.
6. The first player to find all of the signs on the list is the winner.

A typical list might include any of the following:

Arrows-Directional
Bike Route
Caution
Caution Hidden Drive
Caution Speed Bump
Deer Crossing
Do Not Enter
Do Not Pass
Entrance Arrow
Entrance
Entrance Only
Evacuation Route
Exit
Exit Only
Fasten Your Seat Belts
Keep Right
Left Turn Only
Local Traffic Only
Merge
No Left Turn
No Parking
No Right Turn
No Thru Traffic
No Trucks
No U Turn
One Way
Pedestrian
Railroad Crossing
Reduced Speed
Right Turn Only
Road Closed
School Crossing
Signal Ahead
Snow Emergency Route
Speed Limit
Stop
Weight Limit
Wrong Way
Yield

Variations:

You may use an extensive list and then allow players to search for the signs out of sequence.

Or, you may assign point values to the signs with common ones counting for less than uncommon ones, and award the points to the first player to spot a particular type of sign. Each player keeps their own score and the one with the most points at the end of play is the winner.

Car Colors

1. Each player picks a color that cars might be painted.
2. Each player's color should be unique–that is, different from the other players' colors.
3. Play starts with ready-set-GO.
4. Players count how many cars of the color they picked they see along the way.
5. You can set a time limit, set a target number of cars to be found, or just make the game last for the time between rest stops.
6. It's more fun if you eliminate some of the really common car colors: black, white, gray, beige, blue, green, and red. If the players have unusual colors like purple and pink to look for it will make the game more difficult and exciting.

Word Games

No matter where you're from, you use words every day to communicate with those around you. Word skills are some of the most important you will ever learn. But words can be playful and educational all at the same time. Build your vocabulary while you have a blast with these joyously entertaining word games.

Dictionary

Requires: pencils, slips of paper, and a dictionary.

It necessitates bringing a dictionary along, but it's worth it. For most kids a good pocket dictionary will do the trick.

1. Each player in turn will get to be the word chooser.
2. The chooser must find an unusual word in the dictionary that none of the other players is familiar with.
3. The chooser announces the word, and if any player knows its meaning, the chooser must return to the dictionary and select another.
4. The chooser writes the true definition of the word on her slip of paper.
5. Each of the other players makes up a definition and writes it on his slip of paper. When making up their definitions the players should try to come up with ones that seem plausible for the chosen word.
6. All of the slips are passed to the chooser.
7. The chooser reads all of the definitions aloud.
8. The players must guess which of the definitions is the correct one.
9. Each of the players who guesses the correct definition is awarded one point.
10. If none of the players guesses the correct definition, the chooser is awarded 5 bonus points.
11. After each play, the next player in sequence becomes the chooser.
12. A complete round of the game is finished when all of the players have been the chooser once. To be fair, a game should always be played in complete rounds.
13. The player with the most points at the end of play is the winner.

"A" My Name Is Alice

1. This is a fill in the blanks word game.
2. The phrase to be completed is:

   ____, my name is ____________. My friend is ____________. We come from ____________ to sell you ____________.

3. The first blank is filled in with the letter of the alphabet that has fallen to the player and the subsequent blanks, in sequence, are filled in with: a name, another name, a place, and finally the things you are selling. All of the answers must start with the letter for that turn.

   For example:

   A, my name is Alice. My friend is Abby. We come from Arkansas to sell you apples.

   The next player would have to use B. For example:

   B, my name is Bob. My friend is Bernie. We come from Bolivia to sell you baseballs.

4. The game continues with each player in turn using the next letter in the alphabet. When all of the letters have been used, start going backwards through the alphabet.
5. Players are eliminated if they cannot come up with an answer, if they make a mistake in the phrase, or if they use the wrong letter (which becomes much more likely once you're going through backwards.) The game continues until only one player remains.

Variation: Players who make a mistake or fail to answer are given a point and continue to play. The player with the lowest score at the end is the winner.

Hinky-Pinky

1. Player one selects a "Hinky-Pinky"– a rhyming two-word phrase made up of two-syllable words along with a clue to help the other players guess it.
2. The other players in turn must use the clue to try to guess the answer.

   For example:

   The clue could be "My Hinky-Pinky is a reddish metal device used for making corn into a tasty snack." The other players would take turns guessing until one of them discerned that your Hinky-Pinky must be a "copper popper."
3. first one to correctly guess the answer gets one point and creates the next Hinky-Pinky.
4. The one with the most points at the end of the game is the winner.

Variation: Hink-Pink

Played the same as Hinky-Pinky except the phrase is made of two rhyming one-syllable words.

For example:

The clue could be "My Hink-Pink is to put potter's material on a scale." And the answer would be to "weigh clay."

Ghost

1. Player one chooses a letter.
2. Player two chooses another letter that could be the second letter of a word.
3. continues through all of the players in sequence with each one adding a letter to the string.
4. The letter that each player adds to the string MUST continue to form the beginning of some possible word. If it seems that the letter cannot be part of a word, the next player may challenge.

   The player adding the letter will have to name a word that demonstrates that the letter can be used to form a word. If they can't, they add a letter to their G-H-O-S-T (see explanation in step 6), and must select another letter. If a challenge is unsuccessful, the challenger adds a letter to their G-H-O-S-T.
5. The object is to add another letter but keep from forming a complete word of four letters or more.
6. The player that forms a complete word loses the round and picks up a "G" in ghost. The second time they lose a round they pick up an "H," and so on until one of the players has spelled out "GHOST." At that point the player that has accumulated the least letters is the winner.

   For example:

   S

   S-U

   S-U-P

   S-U-P-E

   S-U-P-E-R • *this is the end because SUPER is a word with 4 or more letters*

Word Strings

1. Play is similar to Ghost except that you don't stop when a complete word is formed.
2. Player one chooses a letter.
3. Player two chooses another letter that could be the second letter of a word.
4. Play continues through all of the players in sequence with each one adding a letter to the string.
5. The letter that each player adds to the string MUST continue to form the beginning of some possible word. If it seems that the letter cannot be part of a word, the next player may challenge. The player adding the letter will have to name a word that demonstrates that the letter can be used to form a word. If they can't, they add a letter to their G-H-O-S-T, and must select another letter. If a challenge is unsuccessful, the challenger adds a letter to their G-H-O-S-T.
6. The object is to add another letter and try to have it complete a word of four or more letters that can not be extended by adding another letter.
7. Even if a complete word has been formed, you may continue to add letters as long as they extend the word in a way that could still form another word.
8. The last player able to successfully add another letter to the string completing the word wins the round.

For example:

S

S-U

S-U-P

S-U-P-E

S-U-P-E-R • *This would be the end in GHOST because SUPER is a word of four or more letters.*

S-U-P-E-R-S

S-U-P-E-R-S-T

S-U-P-E-R-S-T-I

S-U-P-E-R-S-T-I-O

S-U-P-E-R-S-T-I-O-U

S-U-P-E-R-S-T-I-O-U-S • *Even though you've reached another complete word, more letters can be added.*

S-U-P-E-R-S-T-I-O-U-S-L

S-U-P-E-R-S-T-I-O-U-S-L-Y • *No more letters can be added and still make a new word, so the round is over, and the player who added the Y is the winner.*

Snip

1. Snip, as originally played, involves throwing a knotted handkerchief to one of the other players. But, in the interest of safety, we will substitute pointing at the selected player, since a travel game may be played in a moving vehicle where throwing could be dangerous.
2. Player one calls out three letters then points to player two.
3. As soon as she points to player two she begins counting aloud to twelve.
4. Player two must name three words, each of which begins with one of the three letters called.
5. If player one reaches the count of twelve before player two can name three words, she calls out "Snip" and the player is out.
6. If player two successfully names three words before the count of twelve, he becomes the chooser for the next round and play begins again.
7. The game may be played as an elimination tournament, with play continuing until only one player remains. Or, it may be better if you keep score since this will keep all of the players involved. Each player is then awarded one point for successfully naming three words, or loses one point for failing to name three words. The player with the highest score at the end of play is the winner.

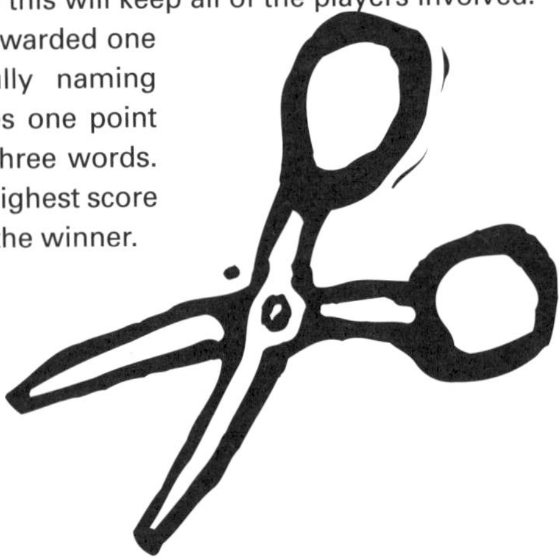

The Woollcott Game

Requires: pencil and paper, and a watch or timer

This seemingly easy game was invented by Alexander Woollcott, a famous American critic and writer for The New Yorker magazine.

1. Player one becomes the scorer. She selects a letter and announces it to player two. She is prepared to keep the score using pencil and paper.
2. The scorer begins timing one minute as soon as she announces the letter.
3. Player two must call out as many words beginning with that letter as he can think of within the minute allowed.
4. The scorer keeps track of how many words are called out with tick marks on the paper score sheet.
5. Play moves in turn to the next player, and the process begins again.
6. In fairness, all players should be given starting letters of similar difficulty on each round.

The following list ranks the letters of the alphabet from easiest to hardest:

S-C-P-A-B-T-M-D-R-H-E-F-L-G-I-W-N-O-U-V-K-J-Q-Y-Z-X

The Minister's Cat

1. Player one begins by saying "The minister's cat is an 'a—' cat."
2. "a—" must be an adjective beginning with the letter "a"

   For example: "The minister's cat is an adorable cat."
3. The next player must repeat the phrase with a different adjective beginning with "a."

   For example: "The minister's cat is an anxious cat."
4. Play continues with each player in turn repeating the phrase with a different adjective beginning with the letter "a" until one of the players can't come up with another adjective, repeats one that has already been used, or uses one that begins with the wrong letter. Play must also be continuous. That is, if a player cannot come up with an adjective immediately she loses the round.
5. When a player loses a round she is given a point, and play continues with the next letter of the alphabet. It is best to eliminate the letters X, Y, and Z from the game since it is so difficult to come up with words beginning with those letters.
6. Once play has expended all of the letters in the alphabet, the player with the lowest number of points is the winner.

Variation: Each player in turn must come up with an adjective using the next letter in the alphabet beyond the one just played.

For example:

The minister's cat is an adorable cat.

The minister's cat is an beautiful cat.

The minister's cat is an cunning cat.

And so on . . .

A Is for Aardvark

1. The first player completes the phrase "A is for ..." using a noun.

   The most obvious example would be "A is for Aardvark."

2. Subsequent players in turn must use a verb beginning with the next letter of the alphabet to describe things that happen to the named subject.

   For example,

   "B bludgeoned it,"

   "C craved it,"

   "D devoured it,"

   "E entrapped it,"

   and so on through the alphabet, and repeating through it again and again, until someone is unable to come up with another verb, or reuses one already played in the round, or uses one beginning with the wrong letter. Play must also be continuous. That is, if a player cannot come up with a verb immediately he loses the round. It is best to eliminate the letters X, Y, and Z from the game since it is so difficult to come up with words beginning with those letters.

3. When a player loses a round he is given a point, and play continues with the loser of the round selecting a new noun beginning with the letter a.

4. Once play has ended, the player with the lowest number of points is the winner.

Categories

1. First a rotation of the players is determined so that each will know when it is his turn to play next.
2. All the players create a six-beat rhythm by slapping their thighs twice, clapping their hands twice, and then snapping their fingers twice.
3. The first player chooses a category and states it within the rhythm, during the snapping phase. The category should be something broad that can include a large number of correct items; for instance: animals, countries, or sports.
4. Each subsequent player must name something that fits the category, and must name it on the beat during the next round of snapping.

A game might proceed as follows:

SLAP-SLAP-CLAP-CLAP-SNAP-SNAP

"category" (spoken while snapping)

SLAP-SLAP-CLAP-CLAP-SNAP-SNAP

"animals" (spoken while snapping)

SLAP-SLAP-CLAP-CLAP-SNAP-SNAP

"lions" (spoken while snapping)

SLAP-SLAP-CLAP-CLAP-SNAP-SNAP

"bears" (spoken while snapping)

SLAP-SLAP-CLAP-CLAP-SNAP-SNAP

"elephants" (spoken while snapping)

SLAP-SLAP-CLAP-CLAP-SNAP-SNAP

"giraffes" (spoken while snapping)

SLAP-SLAP-CLAP-CLAP-SNAP-SNAP

"foxes" (spoken while snapping)

SLAP-SLAP-CLAP-CLAP-SNAP-SNAP

"goats" (spoken while snapping)

SLAP-SLAP-CLAP-CLAP-SNAP-SNAP

"um—" (**we have a loser**)

5. The first player who can't come up with an answer or misses the beat is out.
6. The last player remaining when all of the others have failed is the winner.
7. If you want to keep everyone involved, keep score instead. Give a point to each player who misses. The player with the lowest score when you're done is the winner.

Words from Words

Requires: pencil and paper (except for variation).

1. The object is to make as many words as you can using only the letters from another larger word.
2. A source word, preferably a large one with many letters, is selected.
3. Each of the players tries to create as many words as they can, in five minutes, using only the letters in the source word.

   For example:

   The chooser selects "mountains" as the source word.

   Each player would then create a list of words that are made up of the letters in the word mountains, for instance:

   mount, mint, main, moat, mist, said, satin, stain, ton, tin, noun, tan, moan, mist, and so on . . .

4 Generally, as shown in the example above, letters may be used in a result word no more frequently than they occur in the source word. For, a longer game you may choose to allow letters to be used more than once, even though they only appear once in the source word.

The example could then include result words such as:

maintain, noon, toot, tint, taint, and so on . . .

5 The player who makes the most result words is the winner. Spelling obviously counts. If a player misspells a result word it does not count, and an extra penalty point is deducted from his score.

Variation: If you don't have pencil and paper, or if you just prefer a more active vocal style of game, you can have the players, in turn, name aloud a result word that uses letters from the source word. If a player misses he is out and play continues. The last player able to add a word to the list is the winner.

Word Steps

Requires: pencil and paper

1. Two four-letter words are selected randomly.
2. The goal is to transform the first word into the second word in the fewest possible steps following these two rules:

   only one letter in the word may be changed in each step

   and, each change must make a new word

   For example:

   The words selected are **town** and **coal**

   Player 1 writes

   town

   to**o**n

   too**l**

   cool

   co**a**l

   Player 2 writes

   town

   to**r**n

   corn

   co**o**n

   coo**l**

   co**a**l

❸ Player 1 is the winner because she made the transformation in five steps while player two took six. A player is disqualified from the round for any misspellings.

❹ The letter that each player changes in a step MUST continue to form a new word. If a player wants to dispute the validity of another players word, she may challenge. If a word is not valid, the player who used it forfeits the round. It is helpful to have an agreed upon reference dictionary or an independent party to arbitrate any challenges.

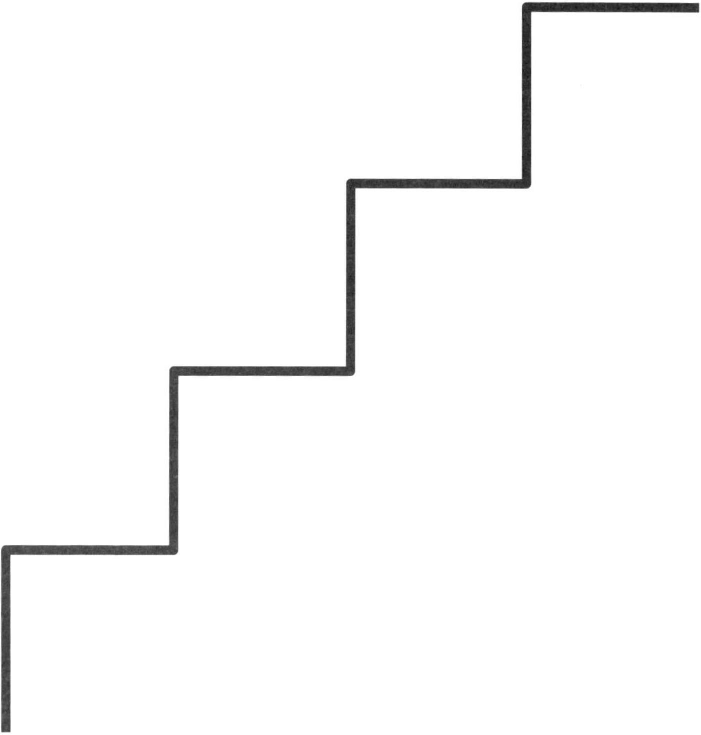

Word Bridges

Requires: pencil and paper for each player, and a watch or timer

1. A six-letter word is selected.
2. All players write the letters of the selected word down the page, draw a line to write on across the page from each letter, and then write the letters of the word up the page, as shown in the following example:

B____________________R

O____________________A

X____________________C

C____________________X

A____________________O

R____________________B

3. Play begins with ready-set-GO.
4. Each player tries to fill in the longest word they can think of connecting the letters at the ends of each line.

For example:

B_______EHES_______T

O_______PERETT_______A

B_______LAN_______C

C_______RA_______B

A_______LAM_______O

T_______OM_______B

5 Limitations regarding the use of proper names and/or foreign words should be established prior to beginning the game.

6 All players must stop when the thee-minute round is up.

7 ***Scoring is as follows:***

five bonus points for the the player having the longest word for each bridge,

plus one point for each letter used in all of the bridges combined (not including misspelled words),

minus five penalty points for any bridges that could not be completed or that used misspelled words.

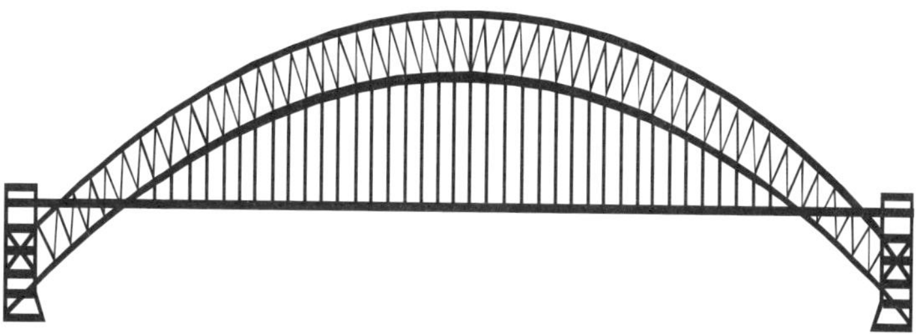

Word Chains

This is a word association game.

1. The first player may name any word.
2. Each player in turn must then name a word that is somehow reasonably associated with the previous word.
3. Adding a new word earns the player one point.
4. The association may be obvious or obscure. An association is valid as long as it is reasonably explainable.

For example:

Let's say the current word is *blue*.

You might associate blue with the *sky*, or with another color like *red*, or with the feeling *sad*, or with a musical *note* from the blues, and your opponents might easily see the association.

But if you said *printing* an opponent might not see any connection and challenge you. You could then point out that a blue is a common term for the proof that is made for proofreading before printing, and so the word blue reminds you of printing.

If a challenge is successful the player being challenged loses two points and the challenger gains two points–if unsuccessful, the opposite occurs, with the challenger losing two points and the challenged player gaining two.

As you can see, challenges are where the biggest scoring opportunities occur. If you can challenge a weak association that doesn't hold up to scrutiny, you can quickly gain an edge. Likewise if you can lure your opponent into challenging a subtle but solid association, you can turn the tables on him and boost your score.

The validity of a challenge is determined by the opinion of the majority if there are more than two players. When there are only two players, it helps to have an independent party to arbitrate the challenges. Otherwise, players must be reasonable and work it out between themselves.

5. The player with the highest score at the conclusion of play is the winner.

Five-Letter Words

This is a two player game, or it may be played with two teams.

1. The first player chooses a five-letter word.
2. Her opponent tries to ascertain the target word by guessing five-letter words.
3. For each guess, the chooser must state two numbers:

   the first is how many of the letters in the guessed word are also found in the target word

   the second is how many of those correct letters are in their correct positions

   For example:

   The chosen word is "roast"

   guesser: beast
   chooser: 3 and 3

   guesser: oasis
   chooser: 3 and 0

   guesser: float
   chooser: 3 and 1

   guesser: frost
   chooser: 4 and 2

   guesser: boast
   chooser: 4 and 4

   guesser: roast
   chooser: 5 and 5 • **WINNER**

4. If a letter in the target word appears in the guessed word more frequently than it does in the target word, the number of matches made is the number of times it appears in the target word. So, "oasis" in the example above is considered to have only three matches even though four of its letters can be found in "roast." The "s" only counts once. Had the target word been "basis," the "s" would count as two matches.

5. No writing is allowed.

Variation: Six-letter Words plays with the same rules but uses a six-letter target word. It is significantly more difficult.

Word Chameleons

1. The first player names a three- to five-letter word.
2. Each subsequent player, in turn, must come up with another three to five letter word that starts with the last letter of the previous word used.

   For example:

   Player one might say coat.

   Player two could follow with tie.

   Player three might then add ember.

   And so on . . .

3. A player is eliminated if he cannot think of a word, uses a word starting with the wrong letter, or repeats a word already used. Play is continuous, if a player pauses to grasp for a word he is out. Play continues immediately with the next player. A player must always pay attention to what the current letter is, even when it is not his turn, since other players going out may pass the turn to him.
4. The last player remaining in the game when all of the others have failed is the winner.

Variation: Players stay in the game but receive a point for any error. The player with the least points at the end of the game is the winner.

Memory Games

Memory games are challenging and great exercise to keep your mind sharp. Many of them give you the opportunity to express your silly side to make the games even more fun.

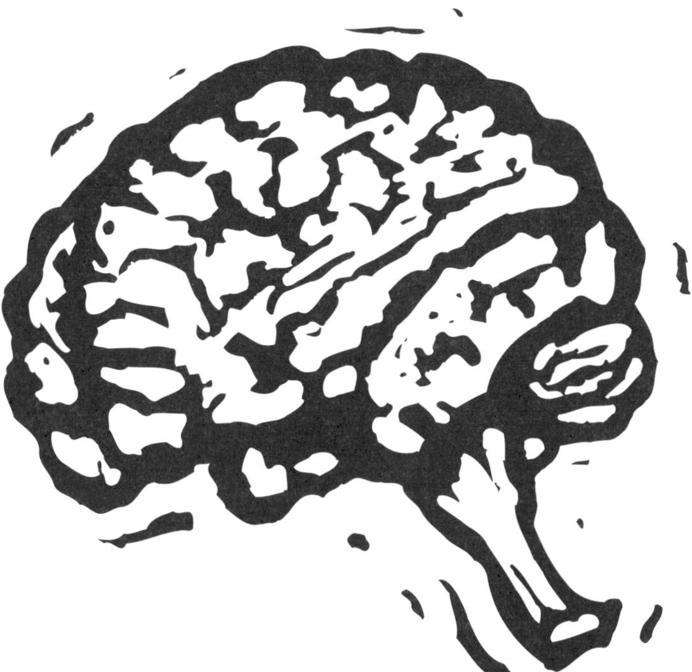

I Unpacked My Grandmother's Trunk

This is perhaps the best known of all the memory games.

1. The first player says:

   "I unpacked my Grandmother's trunk and took out a ________,"

   selecting some item, common or comical that she may have removed from the trunk.

2. The next player repeats the phrase and the item and then adds an item of his own.

3. Each subsequent player repeats the full phrase and previously stated items, adding yet another.

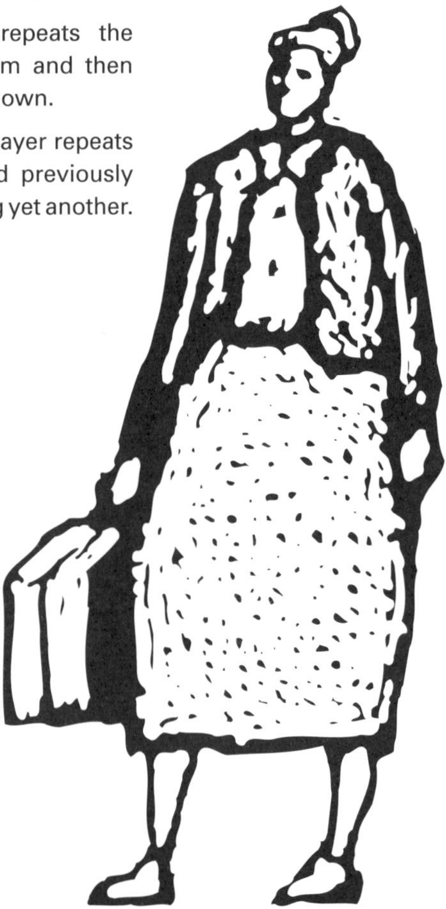

An example might be:

> ***Player 1*** • I unpacked my Grandmother's trunk and took out a comb.
>
> ***Player 2*** • I unpacked my Grandmother's trunk and took out a comb, and a hat.
>
> ***Player 3*** • I unpacked my Grandmother's trunk and took out a comb, and a hat, and a book.
>
> ***Player 4*** • I unpacked my Grandmother's trunk and took out a comb, and a hat, and a book, and a pencil.
>
> And so on . . .

4. If a player makes a mistake, he is out.
5. The last player able to recite the full list is the winner.

Variations: You may decide that all of the items must begin with the same letter. Or, you may decide that each item must begin with letters following the sequence of the alphabet—first A, then B, and so on.

Concentration

Requires: a deck of cards or pencil and paper

1. If you are using cards, separate out the one through ten, the ace and the king of two suits.
2. Keep the twelve cards from each suit separate.
3. If you are using pencil and paper, make two sets of twelve slips of paper numbered from 1 to 12. Make sure that the numbers cannot be read through the paper from the back.
4. Shuffle each of the sets.
5. Lay out one set face down in a grid, as shown below.

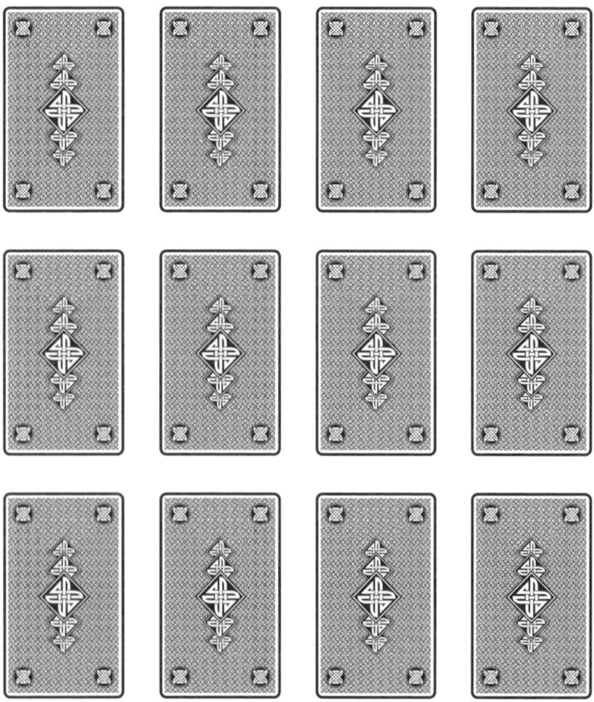

6. Place the other set in a pile for players to draw from.
7. Player one turns over the top card, exposing it for all to see.
8. He may then turn over one of the cards in the grid, exposing it for all to see.
9. If they match, he takes both cards and puts them in his own "winners" pile.
10. If they don't match, he turns the card in the grid back over, and moves the other card from the top to the bottom of the pile.
11. The process is repeated by each player in turn.
12. As the game progresses, players try to memorize the positions of the cards in the grid that have been exposed. This allows the players to know where to find a match when the cards in the deck are turned over.
13. Play continues until all of the cards have been matched.
14. The player with the most cards in his "winners" pile is the winner of the game.

Variation: To make the game more difficult, use more cards to make a larger grid.

What Was that Name Again?

1. Player one says a person's first name.
2. Player two repeats the name and adds a name beginning with the last letter of the previous name.
3. Each subsequent player repeats the entire previously spoken list, and ends by adding another name that starts with the last letter of the preceding name.
4. Names may not be repeated.

For example:

Abner

Abner and Richard

Abner, Richard and Douglas

Abner, Richard, Douglas and Steven

Abner, Richard, Douglas, Steven and Nathan

Abner, Richard, Douglas, Steven, Nathan and Ned

Abner, Richard, Douglas, Steven, Nathan, Ned and Diane

Abner, Richard, Douglas, Steven, Nathan, Ned, Diane and Elliot

Abner, Richard, Douglas, Steven, Nathan, Ned, Diane, Elliot and Thomas

And so on . . .

5. If a player cannot remember the entire list of names in sequence, or cannot think of a new name to add, or adds a name beginning with the wrong letter, she is out and play moves to the next player.
6. The last player able to successfully add to the list is the winner.

I've Got Your Number

This similar, but more complicated, game challenges both your memory and your calculation ability.

1. The game uses only the whole numbers from one to nine, and the mathematical operators: plus, minus, times, and divided by.
2. Player one starts by stating a simple calculation.

   For example, "4 times 2 is 8."
3. Player two must repeat the calculation and add a new calculation that results in a whole number between one and nine.

   For instance, "4 times two is 8, plus 1 is nine."
4. The third player might add,

   "4 times two is 8, plus 1 is 9, divided by 3 is 3."
5. And so, each player in turn must repeat the full chain of calculation and add a new level to it that it still results in a whole number from one to nine.
6. A player is out if he cannot remember the entire chain, or makes a math error, or adds a calculation that does not result in a whole number from one to nine.
7. The last player to successfully add a calculation to the chain is the winner.

Where Is This Going To End?

Another similar game, this one requires a broad knowledge of geography.

1. Player one starts by naming a place.
2. Player two must repeat that place and add a place that begins with the last letter of the place already named. Places should be separated by the word "to," as if describing a trip.
3. Each player in turn must repeat the string of places already named, and add another place that starts with the last letter of the preceding place.
4. Places may not be repeated.

Where Is This Going To End?

Another similar game, this one requires a broad knowledge of geography.

1. Player one starts by naming a place.
2. Player two must repeat that place and add a place that begins with the last letter of the place already named. Places should be separated by the word "to," as if describing a trip.
3. Each player in turn must repeat the string of places already named, and add another place that starts with the last letter of the preceding place.
4. Places may not be repeated.

The Ultimate Memory Game

The object of this game is to create a story.

1. The first player starts by making a simple sentence in which the subject begins with the letter "A." For example, "I am an artist."
2. The second player must repeat the phrase and add to it with a phrase using a noun that begins with the letter "B". For example, "I am an artist from Bulgaria."
3. The third player would extend the story using the letter "C." For example, "I am an artist from Bulgaria. I work with Conte Crayons."
4. And so each player must repeat and add to the story while continuing to work through the alphabet with each added phrase.
5. A player who cannot repeat the full story, or cannot come up with a phrase to add, is out.
6. The last player able to continue the story is the winner.

Variation: For a more difficult variation remove the constraint of following the alphabet and let the story develop free-form.

Pencil & Paper Games

Pencil & paper games can fill hours of fun and give the non-players a break from the noise that accompanies so many of the other games I've described.

Tic-Tac-Toe

❶ Draw the tic-tac-toe grid on paper as shown in the diagram.

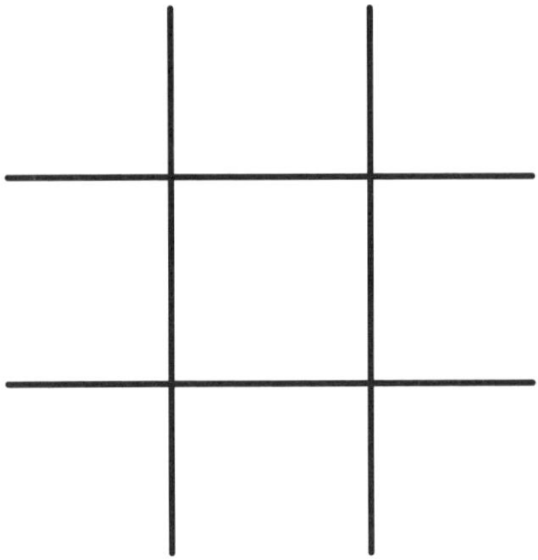

❷ The first player draws an O in any square of the grid.

❸ The second player draws an X in any of the open squares.

❹ Play continues with the players alternately adding Os and Xs to the open squares of the grid.

❺ The goal is to get three in a row (up, down, or diagonally) while blocking your opponent from getting three in a row.

❻ If all the squares are filled and neither player has three in a row the game is a tie.

❼ For a more challenging variation you can add squares to the grid, making it 4 x 4, or 5 x 5.

Dots

1. Make a square grid of dots on paper as shown below. It may be as large or small as you'd like—larger grids are more challenging.

2. Players take turns adding lines to the grid connecting pairs of dots. Lines may be horizontal or vertical but they can NOT be diagonal.

3. If the line that a player adds completes a square using lines that are already drawn, that player puts his initial in the square and then gets to add another line. His turn continues as long as each line he adds completes a square. After the final square he completes, he MUST add another line.

4. When all of the squares are completed the game is over, and the player with his initial in the highest number of squares is the winner.

5. For an interesting challenge, try making the grid in some shape other than a square.

Nim

Requires: pencil and paper, or sticks

1. Draw fifteen lines in three rows as shown:

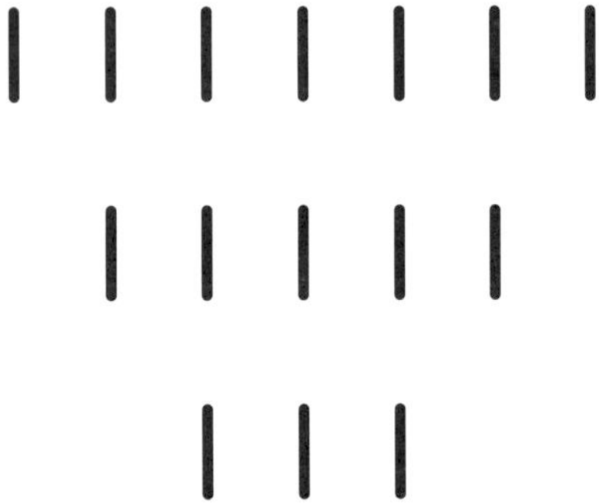

2. The players take turns crossing out some number of adjacent lines in any one of the rows. Each player chooses the number of lines to cross out.
3. You can cross out any number lines as long as they are adjacent and in the same row.
4. The turns continue back and forth until all of the lines have been crossed out.
5. The player to cross out the last line is the loser.
6. Alternatively the game can be played with sticks laid out in rows. Instead of crossing out lines the players remove the sticks according to the same rules.

Variation: To make the game longer and more difficult you may add more lines to each row and more rows to the board. For example:

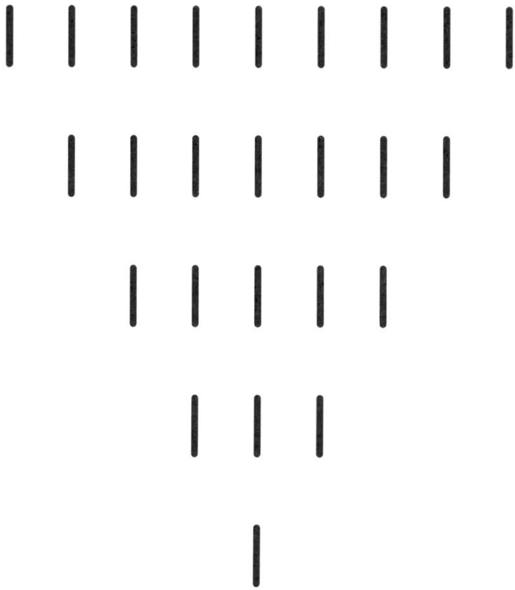

Hangman

❶ Draw a gallows like the one in the diagram here.

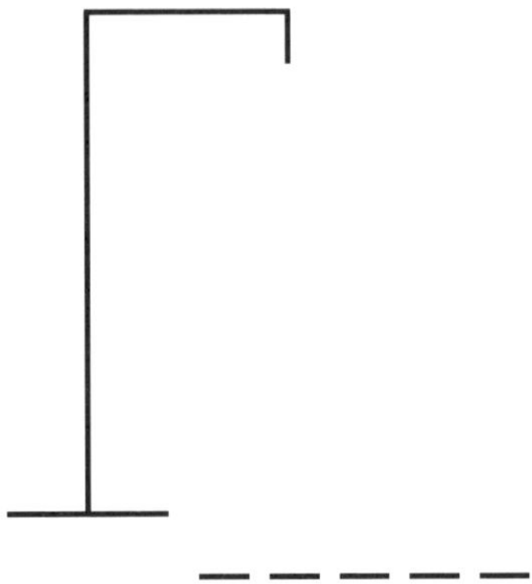

❷ The first player decides on a secret word and marks one line representing each letter in that word on the paper next to the gallows.

❸ The second player tries to guess the letters in the word.

❹ If a guessed letter is correct it is written above the line(s) that represent it on the pavement.

❺ If a guessed letter is incorrect a piece is added to the stick figure on the gallows. First a head is drawn. With each incorrect guess another piece is added: next is the body, then an arm, the other arm, a leg, the other leg, a foot, and lastly the other foot—always in that order.

❻ Keep track of the incorrect guesses by writing them down on any open stretch of pavement.

❼ The object is to guess the word before the stick figure is complete.

❽ If the guesser figures out the word before the stick figure is complete he gets to select the next word and the players' roles are reversed. If not, the first player selects a new secret word and the guesser gets to try again.

Snakes

1. Make a rectangular-grid dot pattern as shown.

2. The first player draws a line between two dots, no diagonal lines are allowed.
3. Subsequent players add a line from the end of the "snake" to another dot on the grid, but that line can not connect back to lines already drawn.
4. The last one to draw a line without connecting back to the snake is the winner.

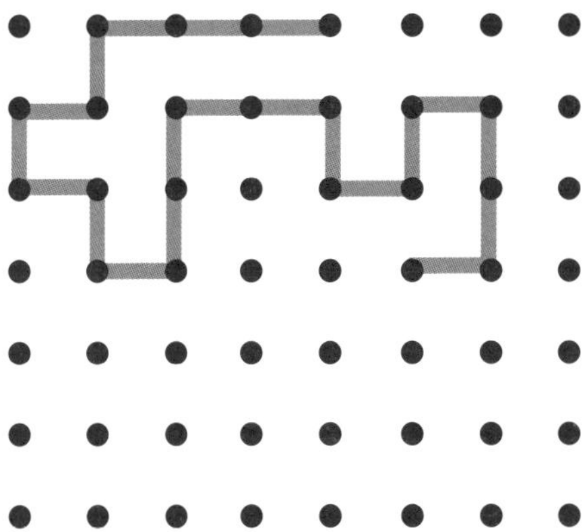

Pipe Layer

Pipe Layer is a two-player game.

1. Draw two grids of dots that are offset and intertwined with one another, as shown in the diagram.
2. One player plays the white dots and the other plays the black.
3. The standard game board has two intertwined 6x7 grids of dots, but you can use more or less as you wish. The long dimension of each grid should always be one longer than the short dimension.

❹ Each players is assigned one of the two intertwined grids.

❺ Each player, in turn, makes a line to connect two dots in her grid.

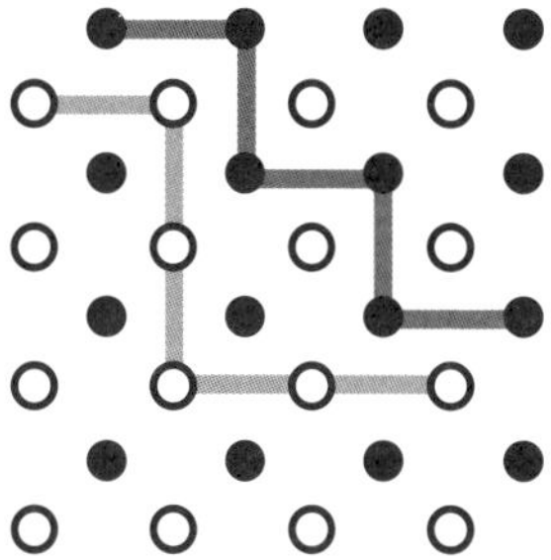

❻ A player can only connect horizontally or vertically adjacent dots within his own grid.

❼ No line may cross a line already drawn by either player.

❽ The winner is the first player to make a continuous line one from one edge of his grid to the opposite edge in the long direction. Note that the long direction for one player will be perpendicular to the long direction for the other.

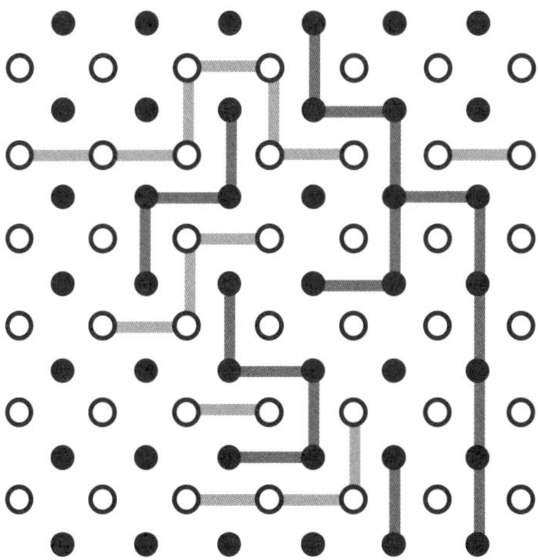

Sprouts

1. Start with three dots on a piece of paper.

2. Each player, in turn, draws a line connecting any two dots on the paper.

3. The player then makes a new dot anywhere on the line he just drew.

4. A new line cannot cross any line already drawn.

5. No dot can ever have more then three lines coming out of it.

6. Note that, since the new dot is drawn on the line the player just drew it already has two lines coming from it. It can only get one more.

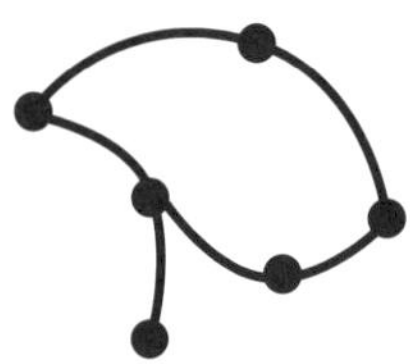

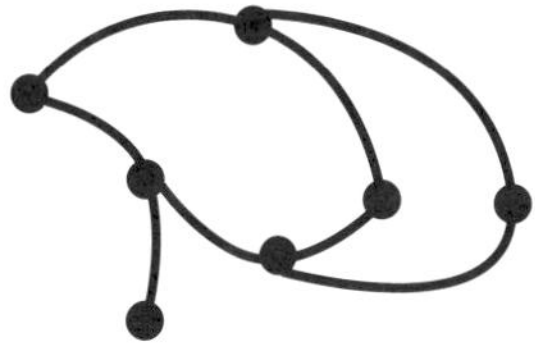

❼ A line is allowed to go from a dot back to itself as long as it doesn't violate the three-lines rule.

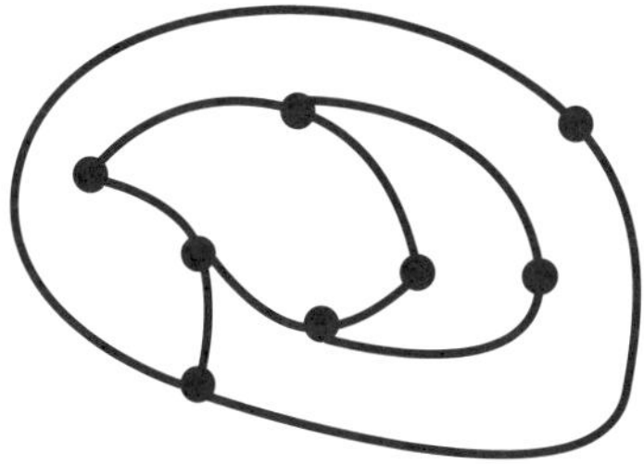

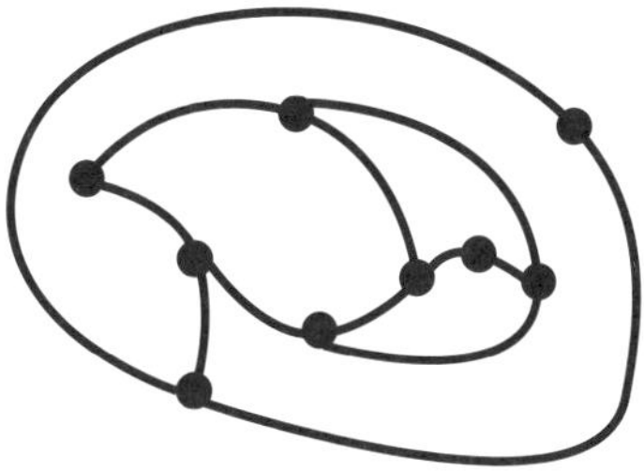

❽ The winner is the last player able to make a to add another line.

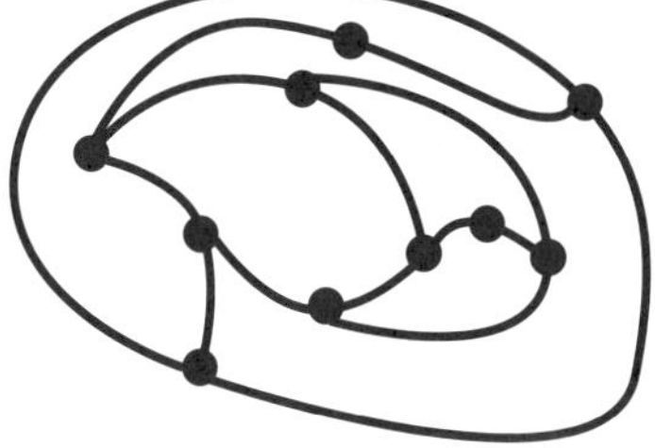

Variation: If playing the three-dot variation of the game gets too easy for you, begin with more dots.

Gomoku

(Connect Five)

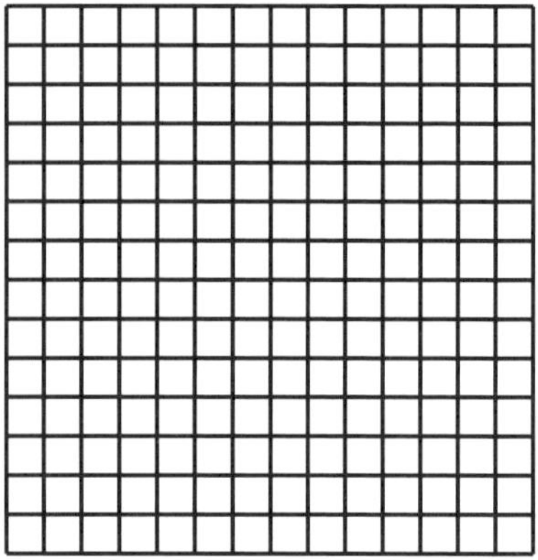

1. Gomoku is played by drawing blackened or empty circles on a 15 X 15 grid.
2. One player is assigned the black circles, the other the white (empty) circles.
3. Players take turns drawing circles of their color on any empty intersection.
4. Black is first to play.
5. The first player to make an unbroken row of five circles–horizontally, vertically, or diagonally–is the winner.

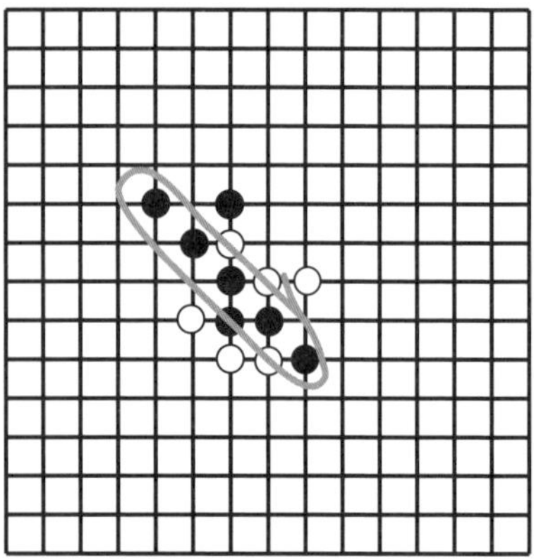

Five in a row wins!

Variations:

By playing first, Black gains a large advantage. The following restrictions, applied only to black, may reduce that advantage:

Black may not make a move that forms two open rows of three circles at the same time (that is, rows that are not blocked by a white circle at either end).

To win black must have an unbroken row of five circles. This row must not be blocked at either end.

Black may not make a move that simultaneously forms two rows of four circles (blocked or not).

Triangles

This game is similar to dots, but the arrangement of the dots is a triangular grid.

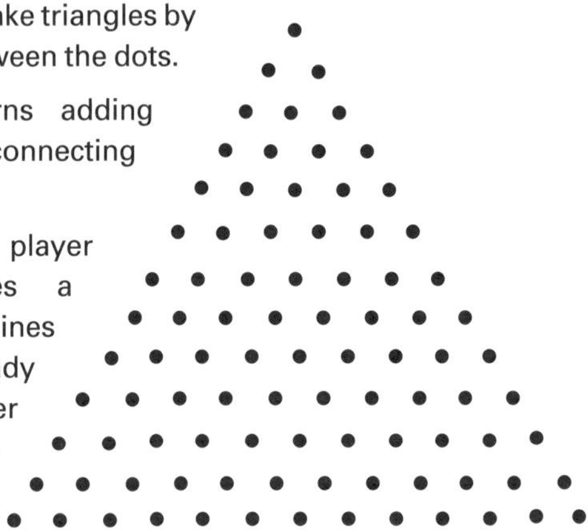

1. The object is to make triangles by drawing lines between the dots.
2. Players take turns adding lines to the grid connecting the dots.
3. If the line that a player draws completes a triangle using lines that are already drawn, the player marks the triangle with his initials and continues to add lines until one of the lines he adds does not complete a triangle. After completing his final triangle of the turn the player MUST draw one more line.
4. In selecting which dots to connect, players are not compelled to complete a triangle even though the opportunity to do so is available.
5. Play is over when all of the triangles are completed.
6. The player with the most triangles at the end of the game is the winner.
7. The grid may be as large or small as you'd like. Larger grids are more challenging.

Battleship

Battleship is a 2-player game, or it may be played by two teams.

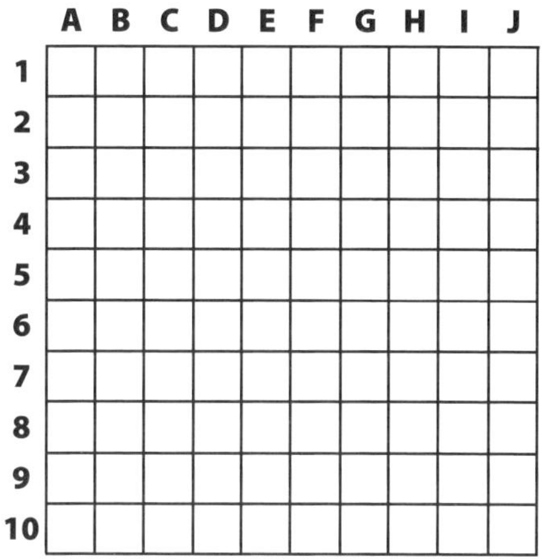

1. Each player draws a 10 x 10 grid of boxes. The grid rows should be numbered and columns lettered as shown. A larger grid can be used to make the game more difficult.
2. Without letting the other player see, each player colors in adjacent boxes of their grid to represent their fleet, which consists of:

   a Battleship made up of five squares

   an Aircraft Carrier made up of four squares

   a Destroyer made up of three squares

   and a Submarine made up of two squares

3. Squares that are vertically or horizontally adjacent may be used for placing ships, but not diagonally adjacent ones.

❹ Once the fleet is placed you're ready for a sea battle.

❺ Each player in turn calls out a "shot" using grid coordinates. For instance, the first player might call "D7."

❻ If any part of a ship in the opponents fleet is in square "D7" she announces a "Hit," and puts an X on that square of the ship. At this point only a hit is announced, not what kind of ship has been hit. The Shooter may want to put a dot in that square on their own grid to keep track of which squares they have already shot at that were hits.

❼ If the shot does not land on a ship square the player announces "Miss" The shooter should put a small "O" in the square to keep track of which squares they have already shot at that were misses.

❽ The turn then moves to the opponent who selects a square to shoot at and calls out its coordinates. The same process of calling it a hit or miss and appropriately marking the squares is followed.

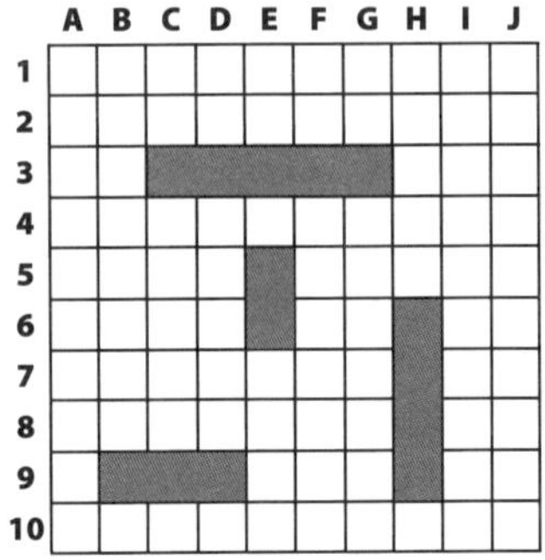

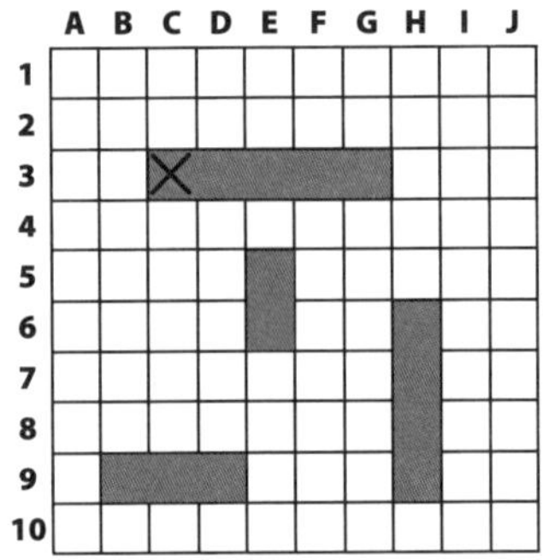

Marking a Hit

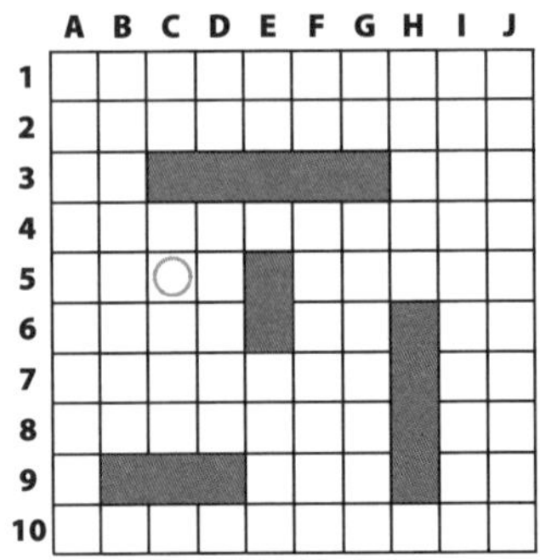

Marking a Miss

9. A ship is not sunk until all of the squares it occupies have been hit.
10. When the final square of a ship is hit, sinking it, the announcement must also include that information,: for example, "That is a hit and it has sunk my aircraft carrier."
11. The game continues until all of the ships in one player's fleet have been sunk.
12. The surviving player is the winner.

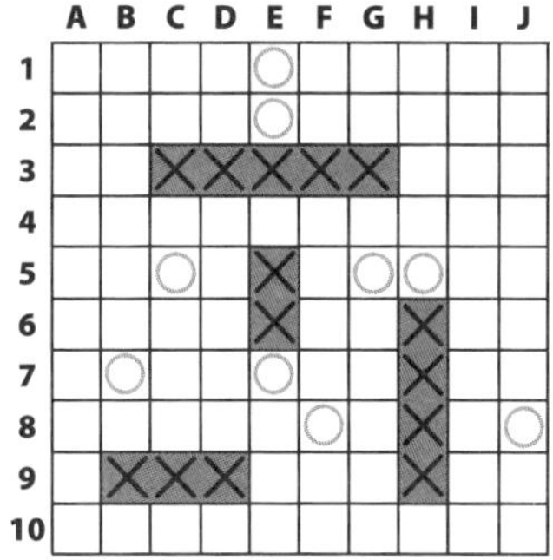

Victory at sea!

3-D Tic-Tac-Toe

1. Draw three tic-tac-toe grids on paper as shown below. Think of the grids as though they were stacked one on top of the other.

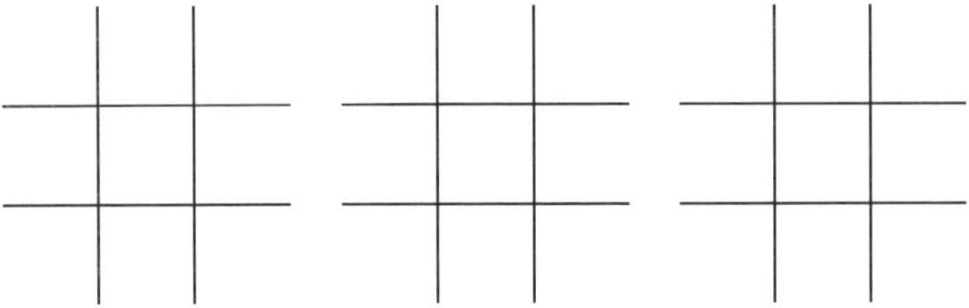

2. The first player draws an O in any square of any grid.
3. The second player draws an X in any of the open squares.
4. Play continues with the players alternately adding Os and Xs to the open squares of any of the grids.
5. The goal is to get three in a row—up, down, or diagonally—on one grid or using all three—while blocking your opponent from getting three in a row.

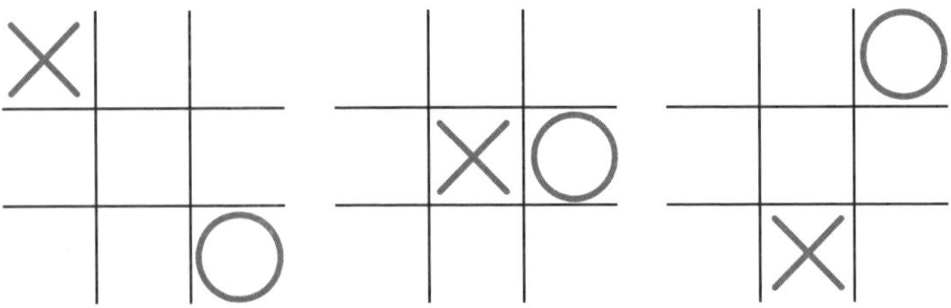

Both Xs and Os show 3-D winners.

6. If all the squares are filled and neither player has three in a row the game is a tie.

Other Games for Travel Fun

Tests of skill, speed, and knowledge round out this collection of games and diversions to while away the time on your journey.

Thumb Wrestling

❶ Players hook the four fingers of their right (or left) hands together such that both hands are clasped tightly, as shown.

❷ On ready-set-GO, the players begin.

❸ Using their thumbs, they each attempt to trap (pin) their opponent's thumb and hold it for three seconds, while avoiding having your their own thumb trapped.

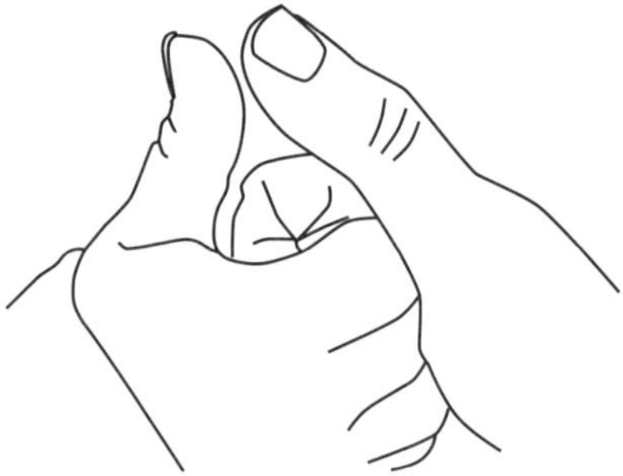

❹ Be aware that the player with the longest thumb has something of an advantage but, just as in Olympic wrestling, quickness and strength can allow the smaller opponent to win.

❺ It is illegal to use any of the other fingers to help gain an advantage for the thumb. Some players will try to use the index finger to sweep their opponent's thumb into position for a pin. This practice, sometimes referred to as "tag team," is strictly prohibited.

❻ It is also illegal to try to use the strength of wrist and arm to lever your opponent's hand into any awkward position that might provide an advantage.

❼ It is important to establish the rules of the count before the game begins. Jumping the count for a sneak attack is not allowed.

Rock—Paper—Scissors

1. This is a game for two players only.
2. The two players face each other, hands behind their backs.
3. Together they count to three and, on three each presents a hand in one of three shapes:

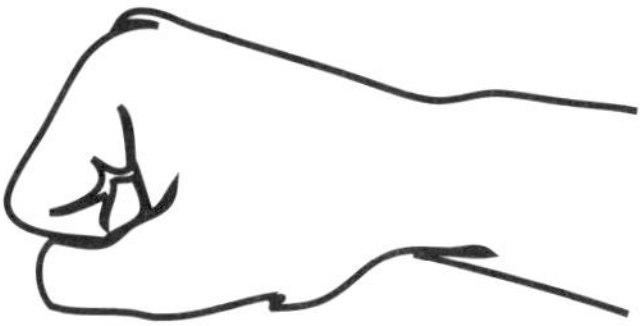

Rock: A clenched fist.

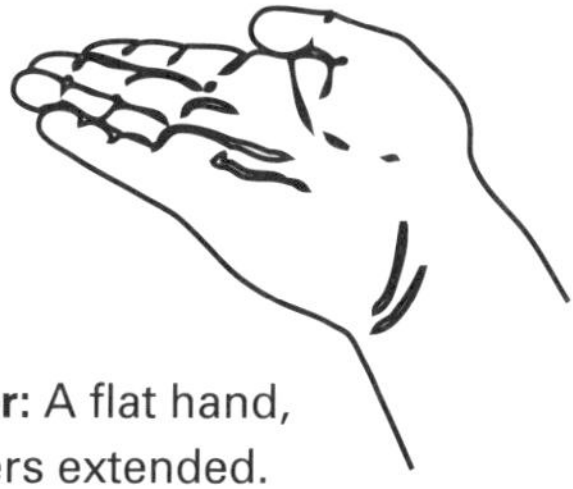

Paper: A flat hand, fingers extended.

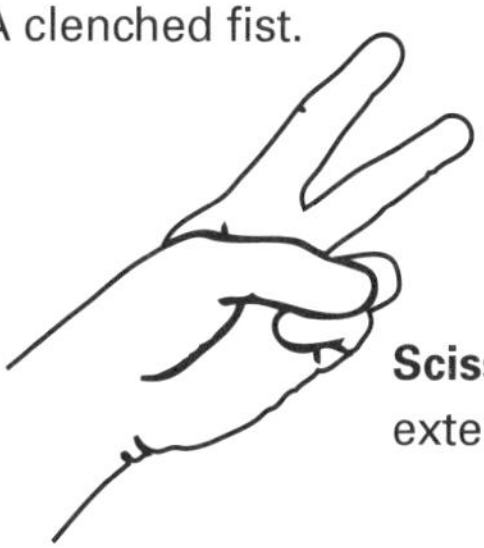

Scissors: Pointer and middle finger extended in a "vee" shape.

4. The combination determines who is the winner as follows:

   If Rock and Scissors: Rock smashes Scissors, Rock wins.

   If Scissors and Paper: Scissors cut Paper, Scissors wins.

   If Paper and Rock: Paper wraps Rock, Paper wins.

5. If both players choose the same shape, the round is declared a tie and they play again.
6. Players may keep score and play until an agreed upon goal is reached to declare a winner.
7. This game can also be used as a selection method in other games, similar to the way a coin toss is used, but requiring no equipment.

Charades

Requires: a watch or timer for competitive play.

❶ Charades is traditionally played in teams, but this individual-player variation works better for small groups.

❷ The object of the game is get the rest of the players to guess the title of the book, movie, or TV-show that you are SILENTLY acting out.

❸ First make a up slips of paper with titles of a variety of books, movies, and TV-shows and put them in a hat, sack, or bowl–anything they can easily be drawn from. Make sure that the titles selected are of an appropriate level of difficulty for the age of the players.

❹ In turn, each player will draw a title and try to communicate what it is to the other players by visual clues only.

❺ ***There are some standard clues commonly used to communicate the basics about the title:***

If it is a ***movie***, pretend to crank an old fashioned movie camera.

If it is a **book**, pretend to be reading a book and turning its pages.

If it is a ***TV-show***, use your fingers to draw a square in the air in front of you to represent a TV screen.

❻ The other players should say what kind of title they understand you to be going for. Confirm that they are correct by touching your nose with your forefinger (indicating they have it "on the nose"). Or, let them know they are wrong by shaking your head, then try again.

❼ Next, hold up fingers to indicate how many words are in the title. The other players should say how many words and you should confirm by touching your nose. The process of confirming is continued throughout the game.

8. Next, hold up fingers to indicate which word you are about to give a clue for.
9. Next, place a number of fingers against your forearm to indicate how many syllables are in the word. If it is a very short word–two or three letters–hold up a hand and bring your thumb and index finger close together. If you are going to act out a word that sounds like your intended word, cup you hand around your ear as if trying to listen.
10. Then, mime a clue to help the other players guess the word.
11. The other players will start calling out guesses based on your performance:

    If one of them guesses the word, point at him and then touch you nose.

    If one of them is close but not quite right, point at them and signal how their guess should be changed to make it right. Chopping the air with your hand means make the word shorter. Pretending to stretch the air means make it a longer version. Waving you hands toward yourself means "you're on the right track, keep trying."
12. The player who is able to communicate the title in the shortest time is the winner.
13. If you don't have a timer, or just want to play for fun, charades can be just as enjoyable without the competition.

Raindrop Races

Fun on a rainy day trip.

1. On a count of "ready-set-GO" each player picks a raindrop at the top of a window.
2. The players follow their raindrops to the bottom of the window.
3. When your raindrop reaches the bottom call out "finished."
4. The player whose raindrop reaches the bottom first is the winner.
5. If your raindrop joins with another unclaimed one on it's way down, the combined drop is still yours—keep following it.
6. If it joins with an opponent's raindrop, it's a "crash" and you're both out of the race.

Challenges

Timed challenges can be entertaining on a long trip.

1. Decide on a challenge that will test the determination of the players. For instance:

   Who can go the longest without blinking?

   Who can stay still the longest?

   Who can hold his breath the longest?

   Who can stay in a particular position the longest?

   Or the drivers favorite—Who can stay silent the longest?

   Use your imagination and make up your own challenges.

2. Begin with ready-set-GO.
3. The one who can outlast the others is the winner.

Can You Name 'em?

❶ Before you leave on your trip, look up and make lists of some sets of trivia that will appeal to your players, like:

the planets of the solar system

Mercury, Venus, Earth, Mars, Jupiter, Saturn, Uranus, Neptune, Pluto

the signs of the Zodiac

Aries, Taurus, Gemini, Cancer, Leo, Virgo, Libra, Scorpio, Sagittarius, Capricorn, Aquarius, Pisces

the Seven Dwarfs

Dopey, Grumpy, Doc, Happy, Bashful, Sneezy, Sleepy

the fifty states

Alabama, Alaska, Arizona, Arkansas, California, Colorado, Connecticut, Delaware, Florida, Georgia, Hawaii, Idaho, Illinois, Indiana, Iowa, Kansas, Kentucky, Louisiana, Maine, Maryland, Massachusetts, Michigan, Minnesota, Mississippi, Missouri, Montana, Nebraska, Nevada, New Hampshire, New Jersey, New Mexico, New York, North Carolina, North Dakota, Ohio, Oklahoma, Oregon, Pennsylvania, Rhode Island, South Carolina, South Dakota, Tennessee, Texas, Utah, Vermont, Virginia, Washington, West Virginia, Wisconsin, Wyoming

the states of the Union (civil war era)

California, Connecticut, Delaware, Illinois, Indiana, Iowa, Kansas, Maine, Massachusetts, Michigan, Minnesota, New Hampshire, New Jersey, New York, Ohio, Oregon, Pennsylvania, Rhode Island, Vermont, and Wisconsin. West Virginia (became a Northern state in 1863)

the states of the Confederacy

Alabama, Arkansas, Florida, Georgia, Louisiana, Mississippi, North Carolina, South Carolina, Tennessee, Texas, and Virginia.

the thirteen colonies

Connecticut, Delaware, Georgia, Maryland, Massachusetts, New Hampshire, New Jersey, New York, North Carolina, Pennsylvania, Rhode Island, South Carolina, Virginia

the countries of modern Europe

Albania, Andorra, Austria, Belarus, Belgium, Bosnia and Herzegovina, Bulgaria, Croatia, Czech Republic, Denmark, Estonia, Finland, France, Germany, Greece, Hungary, Iceland, Ireland, Italy, Latvia, Liechtenstein, Lithuania, Luxembourg, Macedonia, Malta, Moldova, Monaco, Montenegro, Netherlands, Norway, Poland, Portugal, Romania, Russia, San Marino, Serbia, Slovakia, Slovenia, Spain, Sweden, Switzerland, Ukraine, United Kingdom, Vatican City

the countries of modern Africa

Algeria, Angola, Benin, Botswana, Burkina Faso, Burundi, Cameroon, Cape Verde, Central African Republic, Chad, Comoros, Congo-Brazzaville, Congo-Kinshasa, Djibouti, Egypt, Equatorial Guinea, Eritrea, Ethiopia, Gabon, Gambia, Ghana, Guinea, Guinea-Bissau, Ivory Coast, Kenya, Lesotho, Liberia, Libya, Madagascar, Malawi, Mali, Mauritania, Mauritius, Morocco, Mozambique, Namibia, Niger, Nigeria, Rwanda, São Tomé and Príncipe, Senegal, Seychelles, Sierra Leone, Somalia, South Africa, Sudan, Swaziland, Tanzania, Togo, Tunisia, Uganda, Zambia, Zimbabwe

the basketball teams in the NBA

Atlanta Hawks, Boston Celtics, Brooklyn Nets, Charlotte Hornets, Chicago Bulls, Cleveland Cavaliers, Dallas Mavericks, Denver Nuggets, Detroit Pistons, Golden State Warriors, Houston Rockets, Indiana Pacers, L.A Clippers, L.A. Lakers, Memphis Grizzlies, Miami Heat, Milwaukee Bucks, Minnesota T-Wolves, New Orleans Hornets, New York Knicks, Oklahoma

City Thunder, Orlando Magic, Philadelphia 76ers, Phoenix Suns, Portland Trailblazers, Sacramento Kings , San Antonio Spurs, Toronto Raptors, Utah Jazz, Washington Wizards

the football teams in the NFL

Arizona Cardinals, Atlanta Falcons, Baltimore Ravens, Buffalo Bills, Carolina Panthers, Chicago Bears, Cincinnati Bengals, Cleveland Browns, Dallas Cowboys, Denver Broncos, Detroit Lions, Green Bay Packers, Houston Texans, Indianapolis Colts, Jacksonville Jaguars, Kansas City Chiefs, L.A. Rams, Miami Dolphins, New England Patriots, New Orleans Saints, New York Giants, New York Jets, Oakland Raiders, Pittsburgh Steelers, San Diego Chargers, San Francisco 49ers, Seattle Seahawks, Tampa Bay Buccaneers, Tennessee Titans, Washington Redskins

the baseball teams in the American League

Baltimore Orioles, Boston Red Sox, Chicago White Sox, Cleveland Indians, Detriot Tigers, Kansas City Royals, Los Angeles Angels of Anaheim, Minnesota Twins, New York Yankees, Oakland Athletics, Seattle Mariners, Tampa Bay Devil Rays, Texas Rangers, Toronto Blue Jays

the baseball teams in the National League

Atlanta Braves, Arizona Diamondbacks, Chicago Cubs, Cincinnati Reds, Colorado Rockies, Houston Astros, Los Angeles Dodgers, Miami Marlins, Milwaukee Brewers, New York Mets, Philadelphia Phillies, Pittsburgh Pirates, San Diego Padres, San Francisco Giants, St. Louis Cardinals, Washington Nationals

the hockey teams in the NHL

Anaheim Ducks, Atlanta Thrashers, Boston Bruins, Buffalo Sabres, Calgary Flames, Carolina Hurricanes, Chicago Blackhawks, Colorado Avalanche, Columbus Blue Jackets, Dallas Stars, Detroit Red Wings, Edmonton Oilers, Florida Panthers,

Los Angeles Kings, Minnesota Wild, Montreal Canadiens, Nashville Predators, New Jersey Devils, New York Islanders, New York Rangers, Ottawa Senators, Philadelphia Flyers, Phoenix Coyotes, Pittsburgh Penguins, San Jose Sharks, St. Louis Blues, Tampa Bay Lightning, Toronto Maple Leafs, Vancouver Canucks, Washington Capitals

You get the idea. . . Add your own lists of trivia to suit the interests of your players.

2. Have the players each write down all of the answers that they know.

3. You can set a time limit or just keep going untill no one can think of any more.

4. The one who writes down the most correct answers is the winner.

Mother, May I?

1. One of the players is selected to be the "mother."

2. Mother chooses a player and instructs him to do something using the form:

   "(player's name), mother says, (do this)."

   For example:

   "Nicki, mother says, scratch your head."

   Be careful to select things that can be done sitting down.

3. The player must do as they are instructed, but first she must ask:

   "Mother, may I?"

4. If a player forgets to ask "Mother, may I?" she is out.

5. Play continues until only one player remains, the winner.

6. The winner takes the role of Mother for the next round.

Hand Slap

This two player game is a classic test of reflexes.

❶ To begin, players face each other with their hands held out in front of them.

❷ Player one holds his hands out palms up.

❸ Player two places her hands palms down on top of and touching player one's hands.

❹ Once set in this position, it is player one's move. His goal is to pull his hands out from beneath his opponent's hands, and slap the tops of his opponent's hands before she can pull them away.

❺ If a successful slap is made, a point is awarded to the slapper, and roles are reversed for the next round.

The player with the most points at the end of play is the winner.

Which Hand Has the Penny?

This game is great for very young children.

1. To begin, players face each.
2. Player one takes a penny in one hand and placesboth his hands behind his back.
3. Player one may then move the penny to the other hand or keep it in the hand that originally held it.
4. Player one then clenches both fists and brings both hands back in front of him where player two can see them.

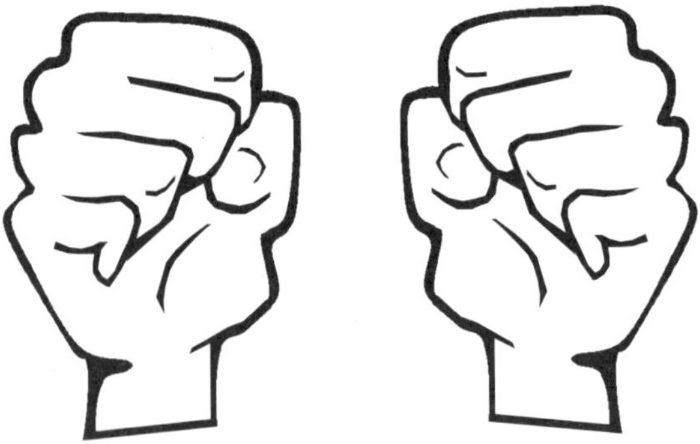

5. One fist contains the penny, the other does not.
6. Player two must guess which hand has the penny.
7. If she is right, she is awarded one point.
8. After each turn the players switch roles with the hider becoming the guesser and vice versa.
9. The player with the most points at the conclusion of play is the winner.